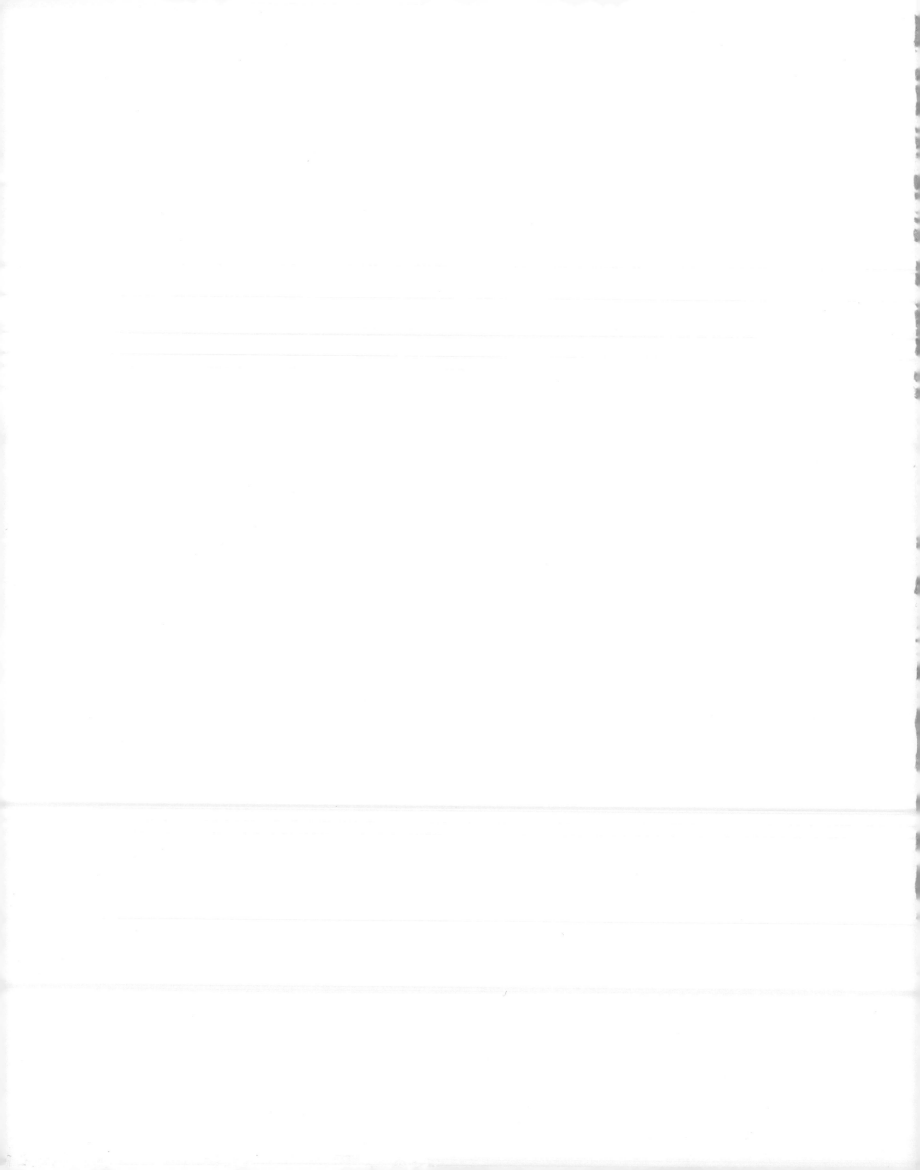

PICTURE PUZZLER

A NATURAL HISTORY HIDE-AND-SEEK

illustrated by

KSENIA BAKHAREVA

written by

RACHEL WILLIAMS

MAGIC CAT PUBLISHING

NEW YORK

CONTENTS

STEP INTO THESE REAL-WORLD HABITATS . . .

STEP INTO HIDDEN WORLDS . . .

Life in the wild is adventurous—and full of danger. From the driest desert to the tallest mountain, animals big and small have learned to stay hidden from prey and predators, finding ways to eat . . . and not be eaten!

CAMOUFLAGE, which was originally a French word, is a skill creatures use to disguise themselves. All of the animals in this book have adapted to their habitats in the most inventive ways.

Deep in a sunlit European beech forest, a furry-eared **BROWN HARE** disappears against the woodland's tree trunks, ever alert to the presence of a cunning **RED FOX**.

Perched beside the Amazon's river basin, a miniature, green **NORTHERN GLASS FROG** conceals itself from the deadliest creatures using its vivid green body and see-through legs.

And on the seabed under Australia's Great Barrier Reef, the **WHITE-STRIPED OCTOPUS** uses its pattern to look like brightly colored coral—something that scientists call mimicry.

Use the clues in every wild habitat in this book to discover animals that use their **COLORS**, **PATTERNS**, or **BEHAVIORS** to survive, and then turn the page to learn more about each creature.

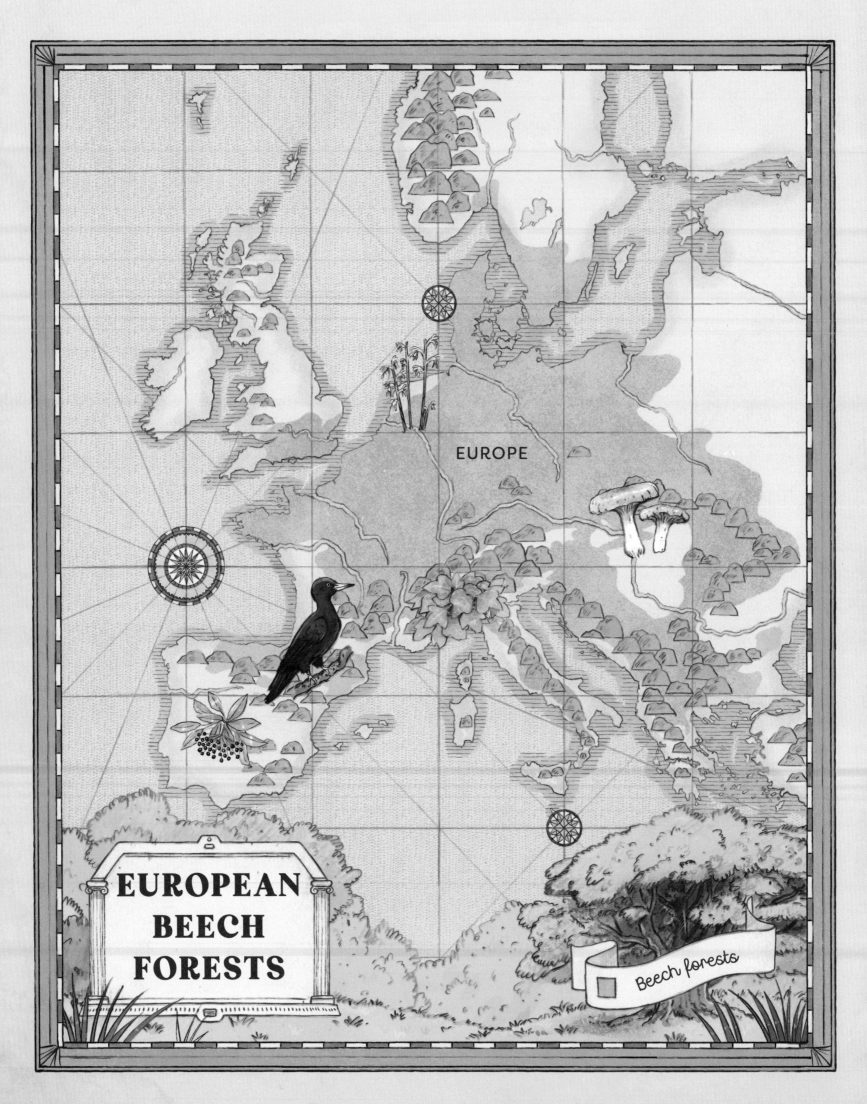

EUROPE

EUROPEAN BEECH FORESTS

Beech forests

FOREST PUZZLE

Hundred-year-old beech trees,
as tall as they are old,
open up their branches
to creatures tired or cold.

So walk on through the forest
and search the wooded glade
for foxes, mice, and bunnies
all resting in the shade.

CAN YOU FIND
these bold, bright creatures?

A wild pony that's gentle and tame. See my dark tail and long, black mane. I'm a **KONIK PONY**.

Dappled shade is where I hide. My spotted coat's a great disguise. I'm a **FALLOW DEER**.

I slither into sunny spots and later hide by leaves or rocks. I'm an **ADDER**.

My striped face is black and white, which helps me stay well out of sight. I'm a **EUROPEAN BADGER**.

I peck-peck-peck upon a tree, to let you know my territory. I'm a **MIDDLE SPOTTED WOODPECKER**.

My big snout helps me root around for tasty acorns on the ground. I'm a **WILD BOAR**.

My feathers make
me hard to spy,
but a bright red line
sits above each eye.
I'm a **WESTERN
CAPERCAILLIE**.

I like to munch on
fruits and seeds.
You'll find me climbing
in a tree.
I'm a **EUROPEAN
DORMOUSE**.

My back legs make me
a fast sprinter.
I shelter in the woods
in winter.
I'm a **BROWN HARE**.

They say that I'm
a cunning creature.
My bushy tail is my
best feature.
I'm a **RED FOX**.

I'm by the water—
a slippery fellow.
See my markings of
black and yellow.
I'm a **FIRE
SALAMANDER**.

Large eyes give me
excellent sight.
You'll find me hunting
through the night.
I'm an **EAGLE OWL**.

Notes on EUROPEAN BEECH FORESTS

HUNDREDS OF YEARS AGO, MUCH OF EUROPE WAS COVERED BY ENORMOUS BEECH TREE FORESTS.

Many of these forests still exist, and their ancient trees are more than a century old. Featuring some of the world's largest and tallest trees, beech forests can be found in eighteen different countries.

Many of the animal species living in these forests are as old as the trees.

DID YOU SPOT ALL OF THE MASTERS OF DISGUISE?

Turn back a page to see if you can find the creatures below, whose camouflage makes them nearly impossible to find.

I have tufts of feathers on my head that look like ears!

EAGLE OWL
Bubo bubo

Eagle owls are excellent hunters. They have hooked beaks; powerful feet for snatching their prey; and great vision, which helps them to see in the dark.

My mottled feathers keep me hidden against the tree bark.

My black and yellow markings warn hungry predators to stay away!

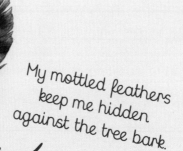

Salamander larva

FIRE SALAMANDER
Salamandra salamandra

The fire salamander is an amphibian, which means it lives on land and spends much of its life near water. Females carry their young as eggs inside their body and give birth to salamander larvae in ponds or rivers.

It's dark and damp under the cool, wet grass near the river. That's just how I like it.

RED FOX
Vulpes vulpes

Red fox homes—called dens—are usually on the edges of forests, near fields where there is plenty of prey to hunt.

My paw pads are furry, which muffles the sound of my steps in the forest.

A rusty, red coat helps me stay hidden from view.

BROWN HARE
Lepus europaeus

Unlike some rabbits, brown hares do not dig burrows. Instead, they shelter in small dips in the ground known as forms.

My long ears help me listen for predators.

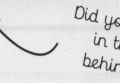

Did you see me hiding in the tall grass behind the pony?

EUROPEAN DORMOUSE
Glis glis

This mouse looks a bit like a squirrel, and its long, bushy tail helps it balance in trees.

WESTERN CAPERCAILLIE
Tetrao urogallus

The female western capercaillie is smaller than the colorful male, and her plumage keeps her well hidden.

I have feathered legs for protection against the cold.

I can cling to mossy tree branches with my large feet and sharp claws.

Turn to page 42 to find all the animals in the European Beech forests.

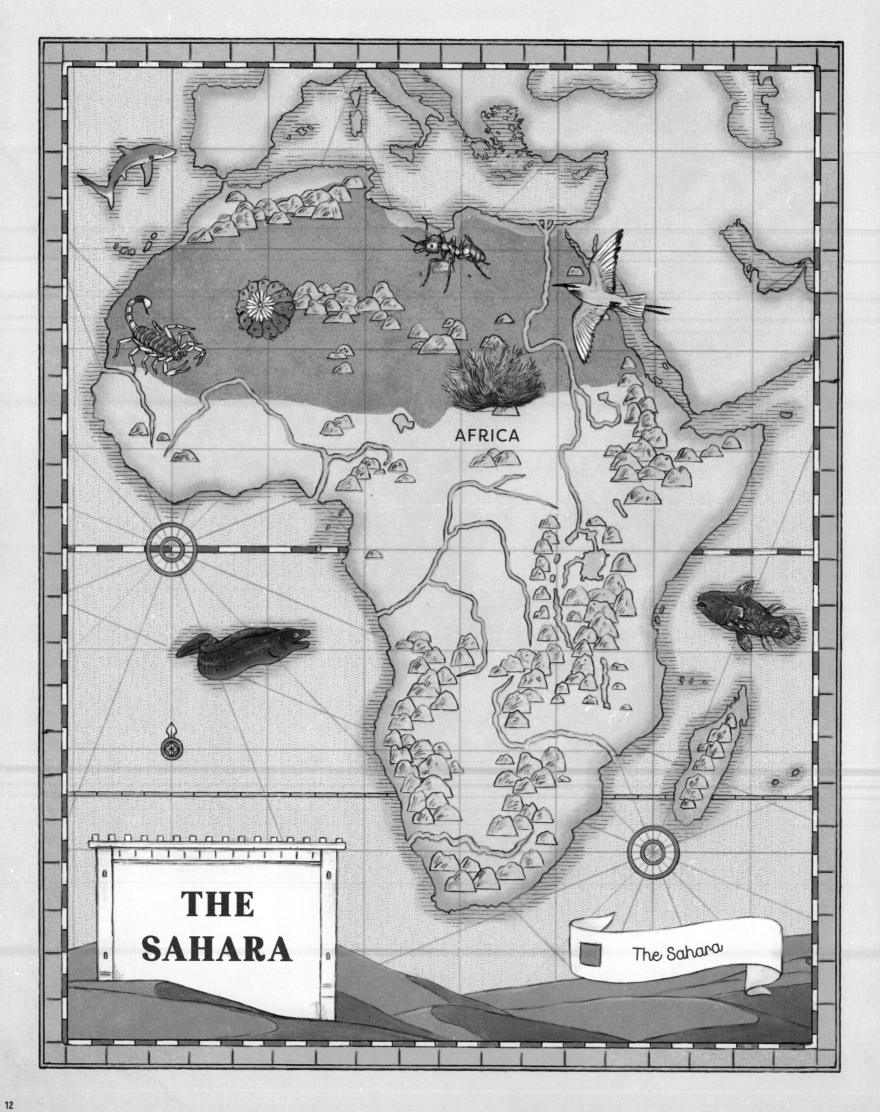

AFRICA

THE
SAHARA

The Sahara

DESERT PUZZLE

Welcome to the Sahara,
where the earth is dry as a bone.
Camels, foxes, and tiny mice
call this desert home.

Get lost among the sand dunes;
search every rock and nook,
for here lurk scorpions and vipers,
if you only dare to look!

CAN YOU FIND these bold, bright creatures?

I may be the world's largest bird, but I can't fly—haven't you heard? I'm a **NORTH AFRICAN OSTRICH**.

I have one hump and two-toed feet. Across the desert I walk in the heat. I'm a **DROMEDARY CAMEL**.

I like to graze on plants and leaves. My long neck can reach up with ease. I'm a **GAZELLE**.

A spotted cat, at speed I excel. My favorite prey? A shy gazelle! I'm a **SAHARAN CHEETAH**.

A long-tailed rodent, I jump so high. They can't catch me even if they try! I'm a **JERBOA**.

Snakes and birds can't eat me at all, when I roll into a spiky ball. I'm a **DESERT HEDGEHOG**.

Large ears cool me
in this desert land.
A yellow coat shields
me in the sand.
I'm a **FENNEC FOX**.

Close to the ground
is where I dwell.
My spotted feathers
hide me well.
I'm a **SPOTTED
SANDGROUSE**.

Across the sand
I like to slither.
My horns and fangs
will make you shiver.
I'm a **DESERT
HORNED VIPER**.

A scaly lizard
with a striped tail,
I hunt mice and birds
and rarely fail.
I'm a **DESERT
MONITOR**.

By day I shelter
away from the sun.
From my stinging tail
you'd better run.
I'm a **DEATHSTALKER
SCORPION**.

I have long horns
shaped like spirals.
My white summer
coat is key to survival.
I'm an **ADDAX**.

Notes on THE SAHARA

THE SAHARA COVERS MORE THAN 3 MILLION SQUARE MILES AND IS ONE OF THE SUNNIEST PLACES ON EARTH.

The long hours of sunshine mean the sand gets extremely hot during the day.
Animals that live here have to be able to survive the intense heat and lack of water.

Many animals that call the Sahara home have perfected the art of disguise.

DID YOU SPOT ALL THE MASTERS OF DISGUISE?

Turn back a page to see if you can find the creatures below,
whose camouflage makes them nearly impossible to find.

Did you see my large, bat-like ears?

My ears help me listen for prey and predators!

Sandgrouse eggs are pale and spotted.

FENNEC FOX
Vulpes zerda

A fennec fox has two oversized ears, similar
to those of a bat, which keep the animal
cool in the daytime by giving off body heat.
Thick fur helps it stay warm during the cold
desert nights.

SPOTTED SANDGROUSE
Pterocles senegallus

Blending in with its surroundings, this bird's
sand-colored speckled feathers are a good match
for the desert sand.

Two horns on my head protect my eyes from the desert sand.

I have a large body and a long, powerful tail. Look for me on a rock near the ostriches.

DESERT HORNED VIPER
Cerastes cerastes

A horned viper spends the hot days buried in the sand or hiding under rocks. It comes out to hunt small mice and lizards at night.

DESERT MONITOR
Varanus griseus

Horizontal stripes on the monitor's tail help it stay hidden.

Did you spot my long, curved horns?

Look for me under a bush near the gazelle!

DEATHSTALKER SCORPION
Leiurus quinquestriatus

Deathstalker scorpions have eight legs and are part of the arachnid famlly, which includes spiders, mites, and ticks.

ADDAX
Addax nasomaculatus

Addax, also called white antelopes, are rare. Their young, called calves, have sand-colored coats. In summer, the addax's coat becomes much paler—light beige or even white—but in winter, it turns smoky gray.

Turn to page 43 to find all the animals in the Sahara.

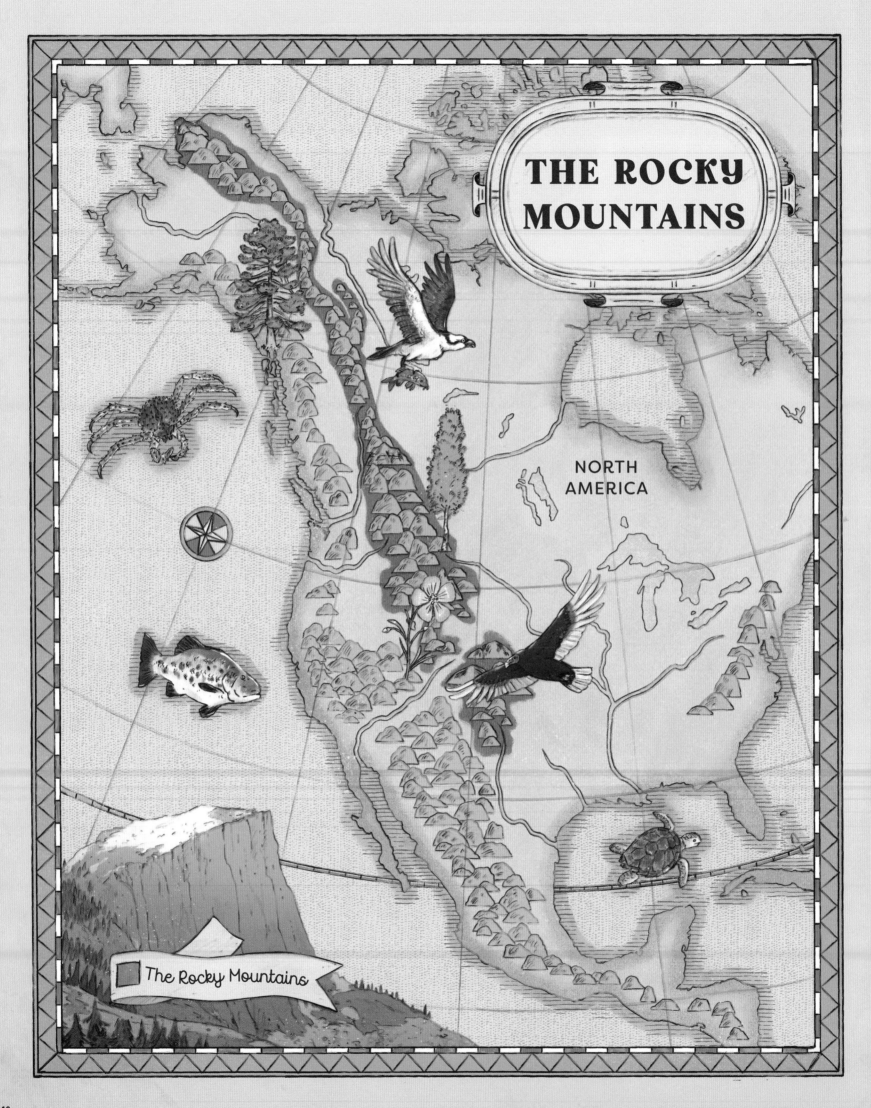

THE ROCKY MOUNTAINS

NORTH AMERICA

The Rocky Mountains

MOUNTAIN PUZZLE

Climb high up these mountains;
explore their dizzying heights.
Find wildcats, birds, and bighorn sheep,
and marvel at the sights.

Majestic creatures roam this land,
though some are hard to know,
like pygmy owls and bright-white hares
hiding in the snow.

CAN YOU FIND these bold, bright creatures?

I'm the biggest cat out here. I stalk my prey, like elk and deer. I'm a **MOUNTAIN LION.**

Knocking on tree trunks I'll be found, Listen for my drumming sound. I'm an **AMERICAN THREE-TOED WOODPECKER.**

I nimbly cross the mountainside. My split hooves help me not to slide. I'm a **BIGHORN SHEEP.**

My patterned fur and my striped face camouflage me in this place. I'm an **AMERICAN BADGER.**

My brilliant eyes and tufted ears help me seek out snowshoe hares. I'm a **CANADA LYNX.**

My antlers grow to four feet tall (though females don't have them at all). I'm a **ROCKY MOUNTAIN ELK.**

NOW LOOK EVEN MORE CLOSELY
for these masters of disguise!

My feathers make me
hard to follow.
Can you spot me
in a hollow?
I'm a **NORTHERN PYGMY OWL**.

In fall, my fur turns
from brown to white.
This color change keeps
me out of sight.
I'm a **SNOWSHOE HARE**.

I'm a reptile—
winter's not my thing.
I hide in tree logs
till it's spring.
I'm a **WESTERN TIGER SALAMANDER**.

With bright, black eyes
and snow-white feathers,
I'm well disguised
in snowy weather.
I'm a **WHITE-TAILED PTARMIGAN**.

I am an intrepid goat,
with horns, a beard,
and a pure white coat.
I'm a **ROCKY MOUNTAIN GOAT**.

Can you spot me
making a dam,
building up
a huge logjam?
I'm a **BEAVER**.

Notes on THE ROCKY MOUNTAINS

THE ROCKY MOUNTAINS, ALSO KNOWN AS **THE ROCKIES**, STRETCH AROUND 3,000 MILES FROM BRITISH COLUMBIA IN CANADA TO NEW MEXICO IN THE UNITED STATES.

These jagged, snowy mountains may not look welcoming, but they are an important habitat for hundreds of animals and contain a diverse range of wildlife.

DID YOU SPOT ALL OF THE MASTERS OF DISGUISE?

Turn back a page to see if you can find the creatures below, whose camouflage makes them nearly impossible to find.

NORTHERN PYGMY OWL
Glaucidium gnoma

The northern pygmy owl hunts for small mammals and insects during the day from its high perches in pine-forested mountains.

I'm so small you'll have to look carefully in the hollow of the pine tree!

You might spot me in the snow next to the small, yellow pine tree.

At the back of my head are large false eyes. This makes me look a lot bigger than I really am!

My large, furry feet help me move swiftly across the ice!

SNOWSHOE HARE
Lepus americanus

In winter, snowshoe hares have a snow-white winter coat to help them hide. In spring, the coat turns nut brown, so it's camouflaged once the ice has melted.

In spring, I stay close to my mate until she's ready to lay her eggs!

Here I am as a baby! After hatching, I have gills like a fish and live in water until I grow into an adult!

WESTERN TIGER SALAMANDER
Ambystoma mavortium

Tiger salamanders breed in water. A female lays up to a hundred eggs, which hatch about four weeks later.

I use my summer and winter feathers to stay well hidden!

WHITE-TAILED PTARMIGAN
Lagopus leucura

Ptarmigans mostly eat buds, leaves, and seeds. They prefer to walk, rather than fly, which explains why they rely so heavily on camouflage to survive.

Swimming close to the river's edge, I can be found busily building my lodge.

BEAVER
Castor canadensis

Beavers use their powerful jaw and strong teeth to cut down trees for branches to build their homes, which are known as lodges.

My hooves stop me from slipping on the ice. Look for me high up on the snowy slopes.

I have thick fur, rear webbed feet, and a flat tail for swimming!

ROCKY MOUNTAIN GOAT
Oreamnos americanus

Male goats are called billies and female goats are called nannies. Both billies and nannies have beards and horns.

Turn to page 44 to find all the animals in the Rocky Mountains.

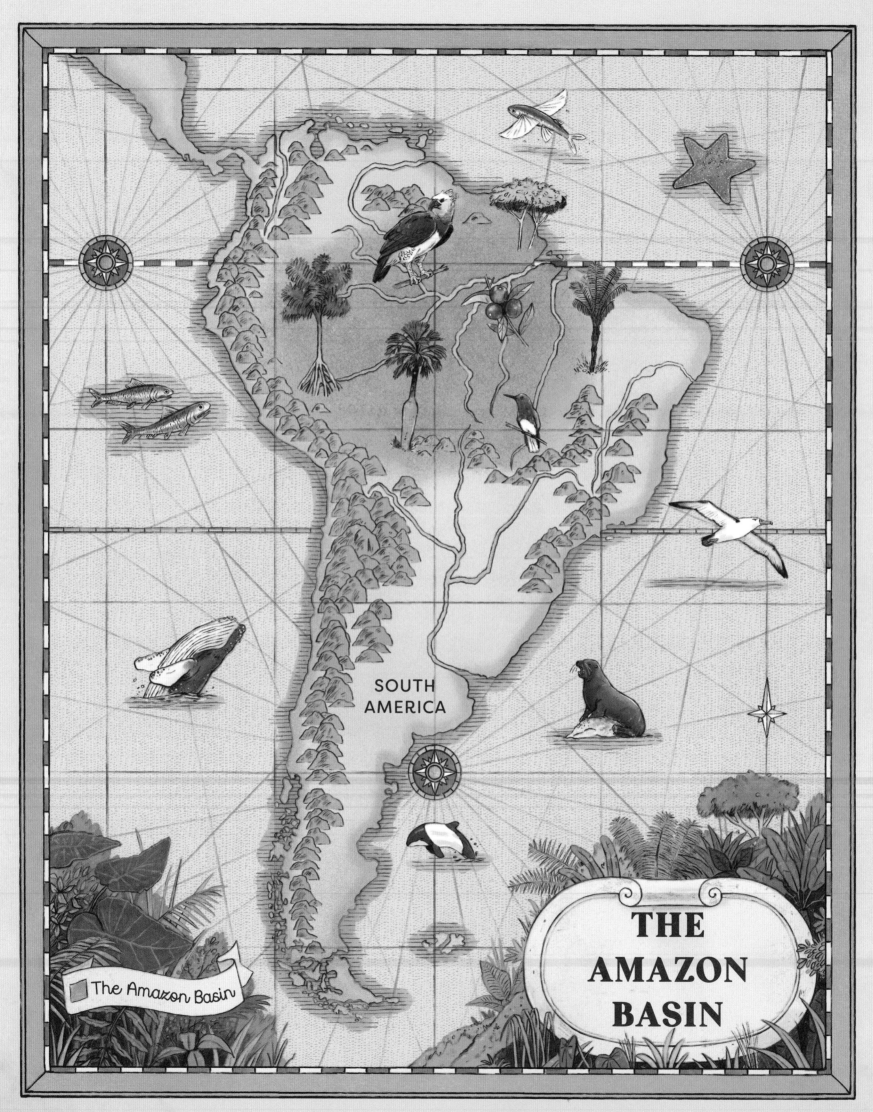

SOUTH AMERICA

The Amazon Basin

THE AMAZON BASIN

RAIN FOREST PUZZLE

In this lush green world
where wild things walk,
find frogs, sloths, and monkeys . . .
and birds that squawk!

Get lost within the canopy.
Scour the forest floor.
Solve this picture puzzle . . .
Turn the page to find out more!

CAN YOU FIND these bold, bright creatures?

A big cat hidden
by rain forest trees,
I use my night vision
to hunt with ease.
I'm a **JAGUAR**.

Atop the water—
watch me flee,
escaping those who
want to eat me!
I'm a **COMMON
BASILISK**.

I'm 13 feet long
and I love to bite!
Who's brave enough
to challenge me
to fight?
I'm a **BLACK CAIMAN**.

I swing up high
from tree to tree.
Jaguars and caimans
can't catch me!
I'm a **SPIDER
MONKEY**.

Perched on a branch,
I sit quite still,
while eating with my
bright yellow bill.
I'm a **TOCO TOUCAN**.

A flutter here,
a flutter there—
my golden wings
are everywhere.
I'm a **SWALLOWTAIL
BUTTERFLY**.

NOW LOOK EVEN MORE CLOSELY *for these masters of disguise!*

I can hide myself
from prying eyes
with tree-green skin
and a clear underside.
I'm a **NORTHERN GLASS FROG**.

See the feathery
tree branch yonder?
"Is it a bird?" I hear
you wonder.
I'm a **POTOO BIRD**.

I'm the tiniest monkey
in these trees.
I'm quick and agile—
you won't catch me!
I'm a **PYGMY MARMOSET**.

In the shallows,
I sit and brood.
Fish and birds are
my favorite foods.
I'm a **GREEN ANACONDA**.

My long neck hides
inside my shell.
Beneath the leaves
I like to dwell.
I'm a **MATA MATA TURTLE**.

I'll tell you now:
I'm very slow.
On my fur coat,
green algae grows.
I'm a **HOFFMANN'S TWO-TOED SLOTH**.

Notes on THE AMAZON BASIN

LOCATED EAST OF THE ANDES MOUNTAINS AND STRETCHING FROM THE GUIANA HIGHLANDS IN THE NORTH TO THE BRAZILIAN HIGHLANDS IN THE SOUTH, THE AMAZON BASIN IS THE LARGEST RIVER SYSTEM IN THE WORLD.

It is covered by the Amazon Rain Forest—one of the world's most important habitats—which is home to at least 40,000 species of plants, 1,300 of birds, 3,000 of fish, 430 of mammals, and 2.5 million species of insects. Many animals that call the river basin home camouflage themselves within its dense flora.

DID YOU SPOT ALL THE MASTERS OF DISGUISE?

Turn back a page to see if you can find the creatures below, whose camouflage makes them nearly impossible to find.

I eat very slowly too . . .

because it takes me so long to digest my food!

HOFFMANN'S TWO-TOED SLOTH
Choloepus hoffmanni

Sloths spend nearly all of their time hanging from branches. Their powerful grip is aided by their long claws. The algae on their coats gives them a greenish tint that provides useful camouflage in the trees.

PYGMY MARMOSET
Cebuella pygmaea

A full-grown pygmy marmoset could fit on an adult human's hand, and it weighs about the same as two boiled eggs. But there is nothing tiny about a pygmy marmoset's tail: It's longer than its body!

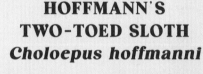

I'm the tiniest monkey in the rain forest . . .

and small enough to hide behind a big leaf!

I'm a bird . . . who looks a bit like a tree stump!

MATA MATA TURTLE
Chelus fimbriata

Blending in with leaf litter on river bottoms, the mata mata is a poor swimmer but has adapted legs for walking on the bottom of its muddy habitat.

POTOO BIRD
Nyctibius griseus

This master of camouflage perches upright in the rain forest's canopy as it sleeps during the day, aligning its body to appear like an extension of a tree's branch.

Spot me in a pile of leaves—not far from a hungry caiman!

GREEN ANACONDA
Eunectes murinus

The spotting on the green anaconda helps it blend into muddy waters. It can lie in wait for prey for hours while almost completely submerged and hidden from sight.

Look closely for my tiny green body. Did you find me perched on a lily pad?

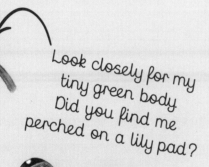

NORTHERN GLASS FROG
Centrolenella fleischmanni

Just about an inch in length, this remarkable Amazonian frog has skin on its belly so translucent that you can see its beating heart and other organs!

Swimming in the shallows, I slither around the tree, hidden from the fish nearby.

Turn to page 45 to find all the animals in the Amazon.

The Great Barrier Reef

AUSTRALIA

THE GREAT BARRIER REEF

CORAL REEF PUZZLE

Deep beneath a sea of blue,
the coral reef sings out,
calling us to look in awe . . .
at what it's all about!

Sharks, small fish, and sea stars
all call these waters home.
So dive into this puzzle—
Earth's rainbow-bright biome!

CAN YOU FIND these bold, bright creatures?

You can spy my black-tipped fins, as swiftly through the reef I swim. I'm a **BLACKTIP REEF SHARK**.

Strong flippers and a teardrop shell help me glide and dive so well. I'm a **GREEN TURTLE**.

Orange and white stripes cover me as I hide among the anemone. I'm a **CLOWN FISH**.

By thick, fleshy lips my sharp teeth are concealed. Sea urchins are my favorite meal. I'm a **HUMPHEAD WRASSE**.

I graze on grass beneath the sea. My baby calf stays close to me. I'm a **DUGONG**.

I flit through the reef like a butterfly. My disk shape and stripes will catch your eye. I'm a **BUTTERFLYFISH**.

Blue spots are all
you'll see of me.
Crabs and fish
just cannot flee.
I'm a **BLUE-SPOTTED
RIBBONTAIL RAY**.

A master of
disguise am I.
Among the coral
is where I lie.
I'm a **BROADCLUB
CUTTLEFISH**.

I'm a flash of green
with orange dots.
Branching corals
are my favorite spots.
I'm a **LONGNOSE
FILEFISH**.

My giant shell
is spotted blue.
Upon this reef
will I stay true.
I'm a **GIANT CLAM**.

Eight wriggly tentacles
give me away.
They help me snatch
and hold my prey.
I'm a **WHITE-STRIPED
OCTOPUS**.

A horse as small as
a fingernail—
curiously, the one who
gives birth is male!
I'm a **PYGMY SEAHORSE**.

Notes on THE GREAT BARRIER REEF

THE GREAT BARRIER REEF, OFF THE NORTHEAST COAST OF AUSTRALIA, IS MORE THAN 1,400 MILES LONG! IT'S THE WORLD'S LARGEST CORAL REEF.

It's home to 400 species of coral, which together form the biggest collection in the world. There are also 1,500 different types of fish and 4,000 kinds of mollusks. It's an important habitat for rare species such as the dugong and the green turtle, which are threatened with extinction.

Many animals that live here have perfected the art of disguise—camouflaging themselves against the reef's bright colors.

DID YOU SPOT ALL THE MASTERS OF DISGUISE?

Turn back a page to see if you can find the creatures below, whose camouflage makes them nearly impossible to find.

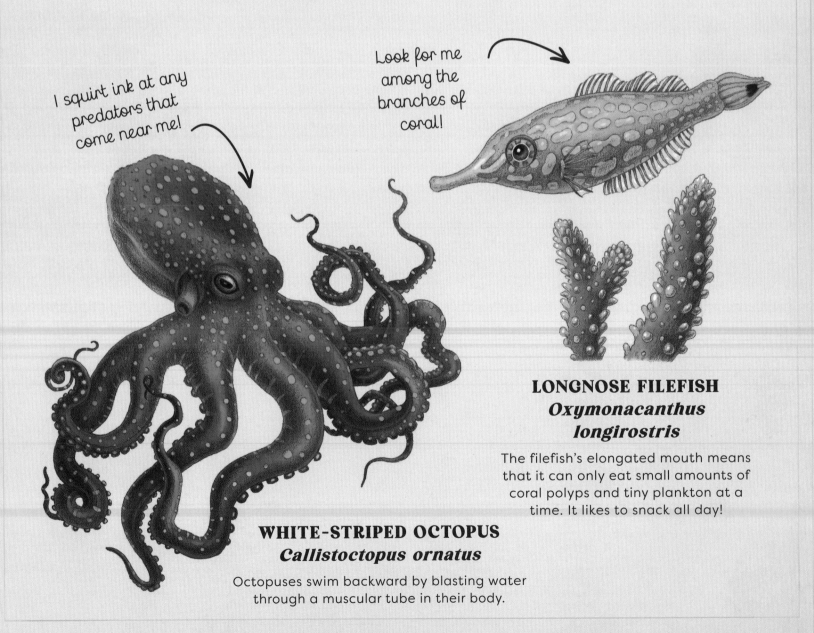

I squint ink at any predators that come near me!

Look for me among the branches of coral!

LONGNOSE FILEFISH
Oxymonacanthus longirostris

The filefish's elongated mouth means that it can only eat small amounts of coral polyps and tiny plankton at a time. It likes to snack all day!

WHITE-STRIPED OCTOPUS
Callistoctopus ornatus

Octopuses swim backward by blasting water through a muscular tube in their body.

Did you find me in the sand, near the dugong?

The nodules on my body exactly match my coral home.

PYGMY SEAHORSE
Hippocampus bargibanti

The male pygmy seahorse can give birth to up to 34 baby seahorses at a time.

BLUE-SPOTTED RIBBONTAIL RAY
Taeniura lymma

At night, the ribbontail ray leaves its sandy hideaway to hunt. It scoops up its prey easily with its snout.

My flat body lets me stay hidden near the seabed.

BROADCLUB CUTTLEFISH
Sepia latimanus

This creature is a cunning predator that hypnotizes its prey with flashing, colored bands that ripple along its skin.

My huge shell is so big, a child could curl up inside it!

Giant clams can live up to 100 years!

GIANT CLAM
Tridacna gigas

A giant clam's bright colors are partly due to the algae living inside its body.

Turn to page 46 to find all the animals in the reef.

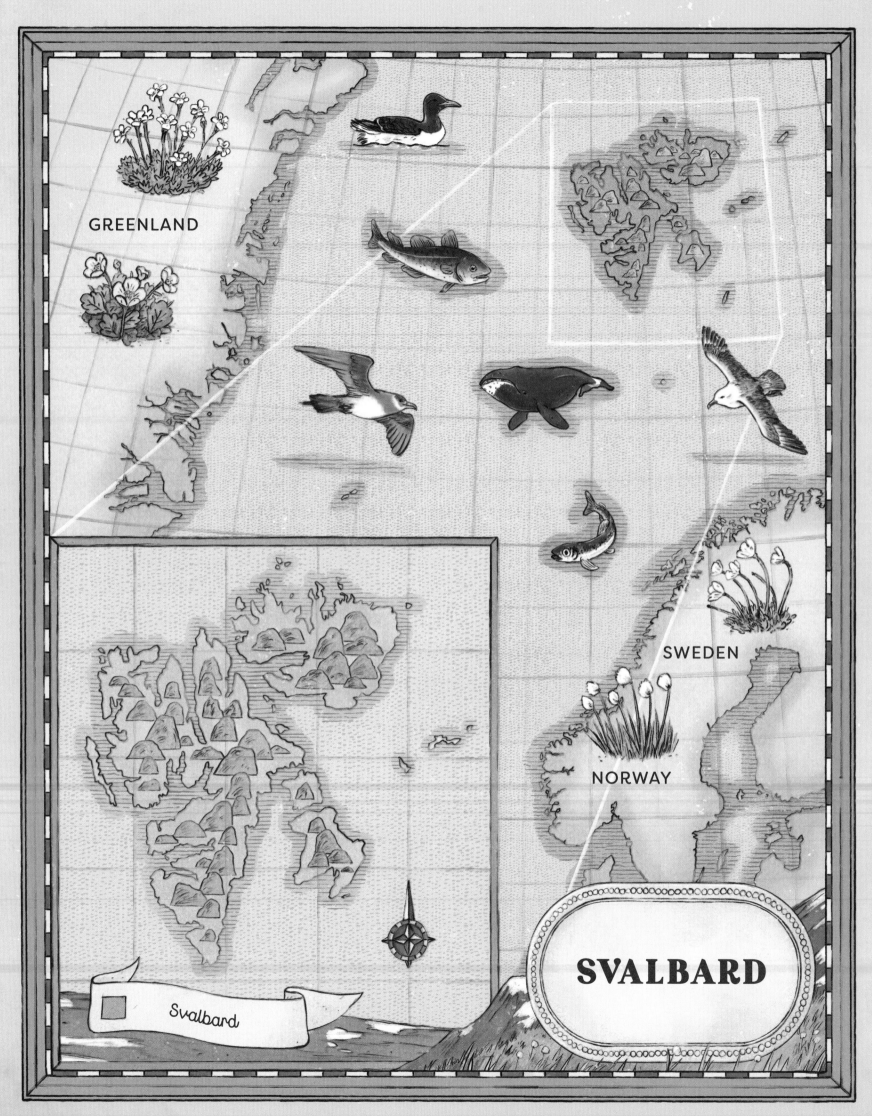

GREENLAND

SWEDEN

NORWAY

Svalbard

SVALBARD

ARCTIC PUZZLE

A rugged land of the midnight sun
and frozen seas and tundra,
where reindeer, seals, and walruses
over icy ground do wander.

Can you spot the polar bear,
with fur so snowy white?
The arctic fox and little auks
have vanished out of sight!

CAN YOU FIND these bold, bright creatures?

My coat is warm and grayish brown. Furry hooves stop me from falling down. I'm a **SVALBARD REINDEER**.

My big flippers help me swim with ease. I rise to the surface so I can breathe. I'm a **HUMPBACK WHALE**.

Two tusks give me power during fights. They also help me climb onto the ice. I'm a **WALRUS**.

Swooping down, I dive quite deep, catching fish in my colorful beak. I'm an **ATLANTIC PUFFIN**.

My large, domed head might look quite odd. I live in a family known as a pod. I'm a **BELUGA WHALE**.

White spots and rings give me my name. Hiding from polar bears is my game. I'm a **RINGED SEAL**.

NOW LOOK EVEN MORE CLOSELY *for these masters of disguise!*

Bright-white fur keeps
me hidden away.
Rabbits and birds are
my favorite prey.
I'm an **ARCTIC FOX**.

I have square flippers
and a bristly chin.
When I spot food,
I dive right in.
I'm a **BEARDED SEAL**.

Like a penguin,
I am black and white.
I flap my wings with
all my might.
I'm a **LITTLE AUK**.

Through icy cracks
I will appear.
My tusk is long,
just like a spear.
I'm a **NARWHAL**.

The arctic fox is a
dangerous foe,
so I make my nest
in places it can't go.
I'm a **SNOW BUNTING**.

I'm the biggest bear,
don't you know?
My white fur hides
me against the snow.
I'm a **POLAR BEAR**.

Notes on SVALBARD

THE ISLANDS OF NORWAY'S **SVALBARD** ARCHIPELAGO ARE KNOWN FOR THEIR RUGGED TERRAIN OF GLACIERS, SEA ICE, AND FROZEN TUNDRA. THE NORTHERN LIGHTS ARE VISIBLE DURING WINTER, WHILE SUMMER BRINGS THE MIDNIGHT SUN.

Majestic polar bears, whales, and seals call this area home
and have successfully adapted to its harsh environment.

DID YOU SPOT ALL OF THE MASTERS OF DISGUISE?

Turn back a page to see if you can find the creatures below,
whose camouflage makes them nearly impossible to find.

My thick winter coat has dense underfur and long guard hairs to protect me from the cold. Look for me near the reindeer.

At night, I keep warm by wrapping my long, thick tail around me like a blanket.

I look a bit like a penguin, but I'm able to fly. See me perched on the rocks near the walrus?

ARCTIC FOX
Vulpes lagopus

The arctic fox is perfectly adapted to the harsh
arctic environment. It is a skilled hunter, catching
geese, seabirds, and even seal pups.
In summer, its fur turns a grayish-brown color,
which hides it in the changing landscape.

LITTLE AUK
Alle alle

In winter, little auks migrate, or travel, to warmer parts
of the world such as the North Atlantic Ocean, and
sometimes as far south as the United Kingdom.

My light-colored feathers help me blend in with the rocks and ice.

At more than 8 feet long, I'm one of the largest seals in the Arctic.

BEARDED SEAL
Erignathus barbatus

Bearded seals are perfectly suited to life in the arctic. Their streamlined bodies and powerful flippers make them excellent swimmers. A thick layer of fat, called blubber, helps to keep them warm.

My tusk is a long, spiraled tooth!

SNOW BUNTING
Plectrophenax nivalis

The vegetation on the tundra grows low to the ground, so snow buntings need to stay hidden. Otherwise, they are easy prey for predators such as arctic foxes.

I spend most of the time living below cracks in the dense pack ice. Look for me with my pod, on the water's surface.

POLAR BEAR
Ursus maritimus

Polar bears are exceptional hunters with keen senses of smell. They can detect seals nearly a mile away.

NARWHAL
Monodon monoceros

Male narwhals use their long, ivory tusks to show their strength and dominance over other males and to compete for females.

I am the largest bear in the world!

Turn to page 47 to find all the animals in the Arctic.

FOREST PUZZLE Answers

1. KONIK PONY
2. FALLOW DEER
3. ADDER
4. EUROPEAN BADGER

5. MIDDLE SPOTTED WOODPECKER
6. WILD BOAR
7. WESTERN CAPERCAILLIE
8. EUROPEAN DORMOUSE

9. BROWN HARE
10. RED FOX
11. FIRE SALAMANDER
12. EAGLE OWL

DESERT PUZZLE Answers

1. NORTH AFRICAN OSTRICH
2. DROMEDARY CAMEL
3. GAZELLE
4. SAHARAN CHEETAH
5. JERBOA
6. DESERT HEDGEHOG
7. FENNEC FOX
8. SPOTTED SANDGROUSE
9. DESERT HORNED VIPER
10. DESERT MONITOR
11. DEATHSTALKER SCORPION
12. ADDAX

MOUNTAIN PUZZLE Answers

1. MOUNTAIN LION

2. AMERICAN THREE-TOED WOODPECKER

3. BIGHORN SHEEP

4. AMERICAN BADGER

5. CANADA LYNX

6. ROCKY MOUNTAIN ELK

7. NORTHERN PYGMY OWL

8. SNOWSHOE HARE

9. WESTERN TIGER SALAMANDER

10. WHITE-TAILED PTARMIGAN

11. ROCKY MOUNTAIN GOAT

12. BEAVER

RAIN FOREST PUZZLE *Answers*

1. JAGUAR

2. COMMON BASILISK

3. BLACK CAIMAN

4. SPIDER MONKEY

5. TOCO TOUCAN

6. SWALLOWTAIL BUTTERFLY

7. NORTHERN GLASS FROG

8. POTOO BIRD

9. PYGMY MARMOSET

10. GREEN ANACONDA

11. MATA MATA TURTLE

12. HOFFMANN'S TWO-TOED SLOTH

CORAL REEF PUZZLE Answers

1. BLACKTIP REEF SHARK
2. GREEN TURTLE
3. CLOWN FISH
4. HUMPHEAD WRASSE
5. DUGONG
6. BUTTERFLYFISH
7. BLUE-SPOTTED RIBBONTAIL RAY
8. BROADCLUB CUTTLEFISH
9. LONGNOSE FILEFISH
10. GIANT CLAM
11. WHITE-STRIPED OCTOPUS
12. PYGMY SEAHORSE

ARCTIC PUZZLE Answers

1. SVALBARD REINDEER
2. HUMPBACK WHALE
3. WALRUS
4. ATLANTIC PUFFIN
5. BELUGA WHALE
6. RINGED SEAL
7. ARCTIC FOX
8. BEARDED SEAL
9. LITTLE AUK
10. NARWHAL
11. SNOW BUNTING
12. POLAR BEAR

FURTHER READING

Illuminature
by Carnovsky

Animalium
by Jenny Broom
and illustrated by Katie Scott

Earth's Aquarium
by Alexander Kaufman
and illustrated by Mariana Rodrigues

Animalia
by Graeme Base

Find Out About Animal Camouflage
by Martin Jenkins
and illustrated by Jane McGuinness

Animal Camouflage: Search and Find
by Sam Hutchinson
and illustrated by Sarah Dennis

How to Talk to a Tiger . . . and Other Animals
by Jason Bittel
and illustrated by Kelsey Buzzell

5-Minute Nature Stories
by Gabby Dawnay
and illustrated by Mona K

The Secret Signs of Nature
by Craig Caudill
and illustrated by Carrie Shryock

MAGIC CAT
PUBLISHING

The illustrations were created in pencil and colored digitally.
Set in Hasthon, Filson Soft, HV Cocktail, and Cursive Script Light.

Cataloging-in-Publication Data has been applied for and may be obtained from the Library of Congress.
ISBN 978-1-4197-7135-4

Printed and bound in China
10 9 8 7 6 5 4 3 2 1

Abrams Books are available at special discounts when purchased in quantity for premiums and promotions as well as
fundraising or educational use. Special editions can also be created to specification. For details,
contact specialsales@abramsbooks.com or the address below.

FSC
www.fsc.org

MIX
Paper | Supporting
responsible forestry
FSC® C104723

ABRAMS The Art of Books
195 Broadway, New York, NY 10007
abramsbooks.com